FOCUS ON GEOGRAPHY

T0014485

Focus on
Cuba

Heather C. Hudak

A Crabtree Forest Book

Crabtree Publishing
crabtreebooks.com

Author: Heather C. Hudak

Series research and development:
Janine Deschenes

Editorial director: Kathy Middleton

Editor: Janine Deschenes

Proofreader: Melissa Boyce

Design: Tammy McGarr

Crabtree Publishing

crabtreebooks.com   800-387-7650
Copyright © 2024 Crabtree Publishing

Hardcover   978-1-0398-1522-3
Paperback   978-1-0398-1548-3
Ebook (pdf)   978-1-0398-1600-8
Epub   978-1-0398-1574-2

Published in Canada
Crabtree Publishing
616 Welland Avenue
St. Catharines, Ontario
L2M 5V6

Published in the United States
Crabtree Publishing
347 Fifth Avenue
Suite 1402-145
New York, New York, 10016

Library and Archives Canada Cataloguing in Publication
Available at Library and Archives Canada

Library of Congress Cataloging-in-Publication Data
Available at the Library of Congress

Printed in the U.S.A./072023/CG20230214

Contents

Introduction

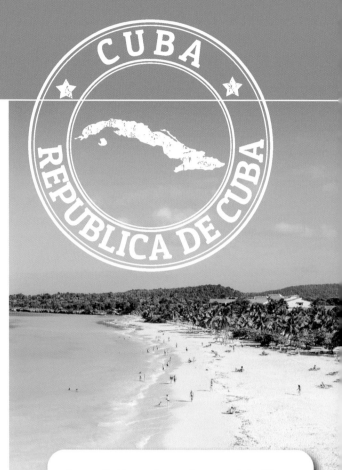

Before the Sun comes up over Havana, the capital of Cuba, it is already a warm 75 degrees Fahrenheit (24 °C) and the temperature will climb another 15 degrees Fahrenheit (8 °C) throughout the day. The year-round sunshine is just one of the many reasons tourists flock to the island nation. But what visitors see as they walk through the city streets is very different from the reality that takes place behind closed doors.

To outsiders looking in, Cuba, an island nation in the Caribbean, is a beautiful country with **subtropical** temperatures and white-sand beaches. The people are warm, friendly, and welcoming. However, life in Cuba is not easy. For decades, people have lived under strict government control. Every aspect of their lives is dictated by their **socialist** government.

Beautiful beaches, vibrant nightlife, distinct culture, and **colonial** architecture are some of the reasons tourists are drawn to Cuba.

More than 2.1 million people live in Havana.

About two-thirds of the Cuban population are of European—mostly Spanish—ancestry. People of mixed European and **Indigenous** or African heritage make up about one-quarter of the population. The remainder is Black, or Afro-Cuban.

Havana's streets come alive each morning with the hustle and bustle of men and women on their way to work. They put in a solid eight hours at their day jobs as doctors, teachers, engineers, tour guides, and more. Then, many turn their attention to the side businesses they run at night to help make ends meet. Many sell goods on street corners. Others hire themselves out as private drivers. Some even operate bed-and-breakfasts for tourists.

Until 2008, all jobs in Cuba were provided by the government. Since then, Cubans have been allowed to earn a private income. Still, approximately three-quarters of Cubans work in government-run jobs. The average monthly salary is just $22 USD. This is barely enough to make ends meet, despite food and housing **subsidies**.

To earn the extra money they need, some Cubans operate *bisneros*, or illegal businesses, such as selling cigars on the **black market**.

Life in Cuba

Most Cuban households have three or more generations sharing a one- or two-room home. Typically, houses are provided by the government and passed down from one generation to the next. People make the most of what they have. It's not uncommon to see couples singing and salsa dancing in their living rooms while their children play baseball or soccer in the streets.

However, housing is a major problem in Cuba. Many homes are falling apart, and construction of new homes has slowed in recent years due to a lack of building materials. These factors have led to a housing shortage. While the government has programs to help homeowners with desperately needed repairs, it is often too little, too late.

Many Cubans dash out of the house each day without breakfast because they can only afford to eat one meal a day. Since the 1960s, the Cuban government has controlled the supply of food. Each family must provide the age, gender, and height of each person in their household to determine how much food they will receive from the government. These **rations** have started to diminish in recent years, however. Private food markets have opened across the country to help meet needs. But prices are high because of the high demand for food.

Hurricanes, such as Irma in 2017, are causing thousands of homes to crumble to the ground before they can be repaired.

A person might be rationed five eggs, 2 pounds (0.9 kg) of chicken, and 6 pounds (2.7 kg) of white rice per month, among other things.

Despite their challenges, Cubans have a strong, thriving culture.

The Island of Cuba

Cuba is an **archipelago** located in the Caribbean Sea. The largest island, called Cuba, is the westernmost island in the Greater Antilles island chain, which also includes Jamaica, Hispaniola, and Puerto Rico. It consists of about 1,600 **cays**, islands, and islets. Together, they have a total surface area of about 42,800 square miles (110,860 sq. km), including coastal and **territorial** waters. This makes Cuba about the same size as the state of Tennessee. Four groups of islands surround the main island. They are called the Canarreos, the Sabana-Camagüey, the Colorados, and Jardines de la Reina.

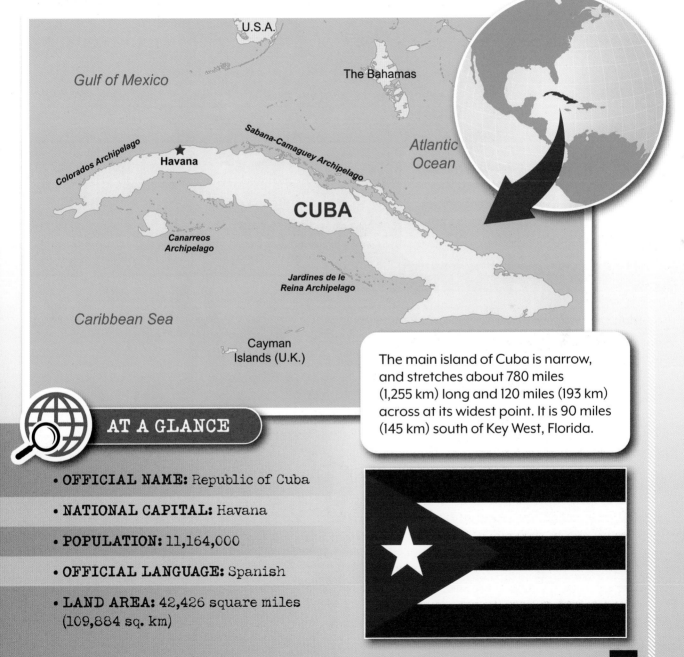

U.S.A.

Gulf of Mexico

The Bahamas

Colorados Archipelago

Sabana-Camaguey Archipelago

Havana

Atlantic Ocean

CUBA

Canarreos Archipelago

Jardines de le Reina Archipelago

Caribbean Sea

Cayman Islands (U.K.)

The main island of Cuba is narrow, and stretches about 780 miles (1,255 km) long and 120 miles (193 km) across at its widest point. It is 90 miles (145 km) south of Key West, Florida.

AT A GLANCE

- **OFFICIAL NAME:** Republic of Cuba

- **NATIONAL CAPITAL:** Havana

- **POPULATION:** 11,164,000

- **OFFICIAL LANGUAGE:** Spanish

- **LAND AREA:** 42,426 square miles (109,884 sq. km)

Important Island

Trinidad is a well-known small town in Cuba. It is a **UNESCO World Heritage Site**, recognized for its historical significance in Cuba's sugar industry.

About 11 million people live in Cuba, making it the most populous Caribbean island. Early settlements were established around areas that were rich with resources for mining. As resources were used up, people began to farm and ranch instead. Settlements soon started to dot the land from coast to coast.

Today, about 77 percent of the population lives in urban areas. Most live in smaller cities and towns spread out across the country. With a population of about 2.1 million, Havana is the largest city. About 450,000 people live in Santiago de Cuba, which is Cuba's second-largest city and an important **port**. Other large cities include Camagüey, which has about 350,000 people, and Holguín, which has about 300,000 people.

These musicians play in the streets of Santiago de Cuba.

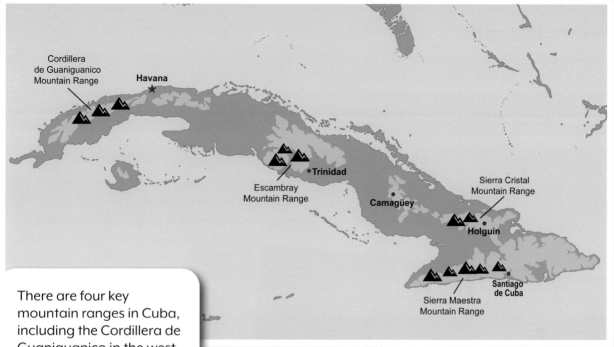

Cordillera
de Guaniguanico
Mountain Range

Havana

Escambray
Mountain Range

Trinidad

Camagüey

Sierra Cristal
Mountain Range

Holguin

Sierra Maestra
Mountain Range

Santiago
de Cuba

There are four key mountain ranges in Cuba, including the Cordillera de Guaniguanico in the west, Sierra Cristal and Sierra Maestra in the east, and the Escambray Mountains in central Cuba.

The Sierra Maestra mountain range spans 150 miles (240 km) along Cuba's southeastern coast.

Natural Landscapes

Each Cuban island has unique physical characteristics. Rolling hills and mountainous peaks cover about one-third of the main island. Pico Turquino is the highest point, rising 6,476 feet (1,974 m) into the sky. Bayamesa Peak, which stands 5,676 feet (1,730 m) tall, is the second-highest peak. Both are part of the Sierra Maestra mountain range. Lowland plains, or flat areas, cover the remaining two-thirds of the main island. The **fertile** land is mainly used for farming and to raise livestock. Sugarcane and tobacco are the most common crops.

Varied Islands

Jardines de la Reina is a protected area that is known for its thriving seagrass beds, mangroves, and coral reef ecosystems. Located about 60 miles (97 km) south of the main island, Jardines de la Reina is made up of hundreds of cays that span about 838 square miles (2,170 sq. km). The unspoiled **marine reserve** is home to Caribbean reef sharks, whale sharks, hawksbill turtles, tiger sharks, and American crocodiles.

Canarreos archipelago is located 60 miles (97 km) south of the main island and comprises about 350 islets. It is home to Isla de la Juventud, which means "Isle of Youth." It is the second-largest Cuban island. It has a surface area of just 934 square miles (2,419 sq. km).

Sabana-Camagüey archipelago is located on the north-central Atlantic coast of Cuba. It is made up of about 2,500 small cays and isles that stretch approximately 295 miles (475 km). 35 protected sites are found there, such as reserves and national parks.

At just 62 miles (100 km) long, the Colorados archipelago is made up of smaller cays and isles along Cuba's northwestern coast. It is mainly known for its tourism and **commercial** fishing industries.

Caribbean reef shark

Jardines de la Reina translates to "queen's gardens."

Isla de la Juventud is home to almost 85,000 people. It is also a tourist destination.

Ranchers mainly raise cattle, pigs, and chickens.

Land Use

About 80 percent of Cuba's food is imported from other countries. Still, farming continues to be a major industry in Cuba, and it accounts for about 20 percent of the labor force. For centuries, coffee and tobacco have competed with sugarcane as Cuba's most important crops. Other common crops include rice, citrus fruits, plantains, cassava, and corn. Pricing and production is controlled by the Cuban government. Fuel shortages and a lack of access to modern farming equipment pose major challenges for farmers. Many rely on manual labor and animal power to work the land.

Closer Look

Resource-Rich

Cuba has significant petroleum and mineral resources. It is one of the top 10 countries for cobalt and nickel production. Other resources include hydroelectric power, **arable** land, iron ore, salt, timber, copper, chromium, magnetite, manganese, and natural gas.

Forests cover about one-quarter of Cuba's land.

Water World

As an island nation, Cuba has 3,570 miles (5,745 km) of coastline. The country is known for its soft-sand beaches and pristine coastal waters, which are said to be some of the finest in the world. However, inland waters are few. There are some small freshwater lakes and saltwater lagoons. At about 25 square miles (66 sq. km), Laguna de la Leche, or "Milk Lake," is the largest natural lake in Cuba.

There are also about 600 short rivers and streams across Cuba. The longest, Cauto River, extends 230 miles (370 km) westward from the Sierra Maestra mountains to the Gulf of Guacanayabo. Although the river cannot be used for drinking, the fertile land around it is used for farming sugarcane, rice, and tobacco.

The Toa is often called the mightiest river in Cuba. It has 72 **tributaries** and is home to 1,000 flower species.

Gypsum and limestone deposits give Laguna de la Leche its murky, milky appearance.

Aquaculture is a growing industry in Cuba. It involves farming fish and other wildlife, usually for humans to eat.

Fruitful Waters

Fishing provides jobs for about 50,000 people in Cuba's coastal communities. The country is known for its marine diversity, making it a top seafood supplier for countries around the world. Fishing creates income for locals and also serves as an important source of food for many families.

Cienfuegos Bay, on the south coast of Cuba, serves as a harbor for fishing and other boats. It is also home to one of the main ports in Cuba.

Tuna, hake, lobster, shellfish, and needlefish are common catches among the country's more than 100 commercial species. However, overfishing has become a problem in Cuba. Estimates suggest about 60 percent of commercial species are overfished. Overfishing can also lead to the deterioration of Cuba's important coral reefs. The country has established science and conservation programs to help combat the issue.

As hurricanes become more frequent and intense due to **climate change**, the government has started building hurricane-resistant housing.

Tropical Temperatures

Cuba has a subtropical climate with an average temperature of 79 degrees Fahrenheit (26 °C). Summer temperatures reach up to 85 degrees Fahrenheit (29 °C), while winter temperatures dip down to about 70 degrees Fahrenheit (21 °C). The average humidity is 60 to 70 percent during the day and 80 to 90 percent at night. There are two seasons in Cuba. The country receives about three-quarters of its annual precipitation during the rainy season, which takes place between May and October. The dry season happens from November to April, and droughts, or long periods without rainfall, are common. Hurricane season starts in June and ends in November. It can bring harsh, damaging storms. In September 2022, for example, Hurricane Ian damaged more than 100,000 homes.

Spectacular Species

Cuba is home to more than 6,000 plant species. About half cannot be found any other place on Earth, including beautiful flowering plants such as some orchid species. Some of the tree species found in Cuba include piñón trees, cork palms, and royal palms.

Animal life is abundant across Cuba. There are more than 300 bird species, 500 fish species, and 7,000 insect species. Cuban crocodiles, Caribbean manatees, whale sharks, and hawksbill turtles are some of the creatures living in Cuba's waters. The Cuban ivory-billed woodpecker, Cuban tody, and giant kingbird can be found in Cuba's skies. Cuban ground iguanas, land crabs, and Cuban spotted toads are some of the other animals that call Cuba home. There are also about 30 types of mammals, including bats, solenodons, and Cuban hutias.

The white mariposa, or butterfly jasmine, is Cuba's national flower.

Cuba has many protected areas dedicated to the preservation of the country's culture, land, and animals. They include the UNESCO World Heritage Sites of Viñales Valley, which is known for its **karst** landscape and traditional agricultural practices, and Desembarco del Granma National Park, which features coral reefs and **submarine terraces**.

Viñales Valley is found in western Cuba.

The smallest bird in the world, the bee hummingbird, is found only in Cuba.

Building a Nation

Cuban history dates back long before the arrival of Christopher Columbus in the Americas in the 15th century. Evidence of human life in the country now known as Cuba dates back to 4000 B.C.E. Indigenous peoples there belonged to several groups. Each had its own language, culture, and ways of life.

Earliest Arrivals

The Guanahatabey and the Ciboney, which included the Cayo Redondo or Guayabo Blanco cultures, were some of the earliest known people to inhabit the land now known as Cuba.

The Guanahatabey arrived first, and it is believed they came from the southern part of what is now the United States. They were gatherers who survived mainly on fruit and mollusks. They made shell tools and lived in caves and rock shelters. Many of these ancient sites are now submerged underwater.

The Ciboney migrated to Cuba from South America. Language similarities make scholars believe that they were a subgroup of the Taíno people (see opposite page). They hunted, fished, and used basic farming methods. They also made shell tools and ate foods such as mollusks, rodents, fish, birds, and turtles.

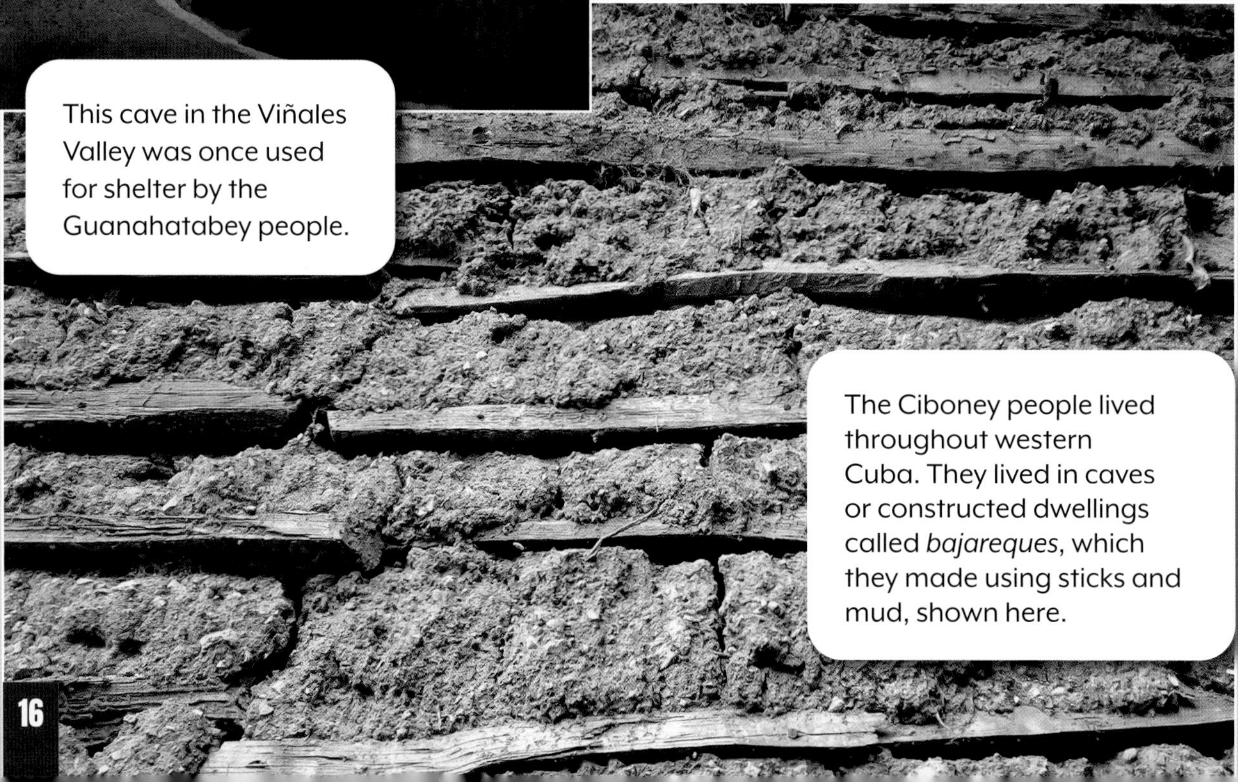

This cave in the Viñales Valley was once used for shelter by the Guanahatabey people.

The Ciboney people lived throughout western Cuba. They lived in caves or constructed dwellings called *bajareques*, which they made using sticks and mud, shown here.

Taíno homes were made of palm trees, as shown by these reconstructions in Zapata National Park in south-central Cuba.

Cuban performers keep Taíno culture alive near Cueva del Indio in Viñales Valley, the site of an ancient Indigenous settlement.

Taíno Culture

The Taíno migrated to Cuba around 500 C.E. and were widespread across the Caribbean. They settled in villages and lived in round houses near freshwater sources in the central and eastern parts of Cuba. The Taíno practiced more sophisticated farming methods. Corn, yuca, cotton, and tobacco were some of their most important crops. They built wooden canoes to carry them across the water. They also had a class system that helped organize their society. Over time, the Taíno spread across Cuba and pushed most of the other cultures off the island. By the time Columbus arrived in 1492, they accounted for about 90 percent of the population of the land now called Cuba.

Europeans Arrive

In 1492, Italian explorer Christopher Columbus was commissioned by the Spanish king to search for a direct route between Europe and Asia. He set sail in late August and arrived on the northern coast of Cuba in October of that year. He called the island Juana and claimed it for Spain. This event forever changed the course of history for the island's original inhabitants.

Spanish Colonialism

It was 19 years before the first permanent Spanish settlement was established on the island. **Conquistador** Diego Velázquez de Cuéllar led the effort to build a community near Baracoa. Other settlements, such as Santiago de Cuba and Havana, came to follow over the next few years. The Spanish quickly set up a system of government made up of elected representatives from each town council. A legal system called *encomienda* gave the Spanish control over the island's Indigenous peoples. They were required to convert to Christianity and perform forced labor or make payments to conquistadors.

The *encomienda* system was a way for Spain to enslave Indigenous peoples as laborers in the regions they conquered.

As the oldest city in Cuba, Baracoa is often called the First City. It was originally a Taíno settlement.

Indigenous and Early African Enslavement

Thousands of Indigenous peoples died from infectious diseases brought by the Spanish and the harsh, abusive living conditions under Spanish control. Many fled to the mountains. Within the first century of Spanish colonialism, few of the island's first peoples remained.

The first enslaved Africans came to Juana with early Spanish settlers. However, with a shortage of laborers due to the dwindling Indigenous population, the Spanish settlers needed to find more people to mine gold and farm the land. They looked to African laborers to fill the gap. By the 1520s, large groups of enslaved Africans were being brought to Juana.

Many people with Taíno ancestry today are descended from those who fled to hidden settlements in the Cuban mountains.

Artifacts from the **slave trade** are displayed at an old coffee plantation near Santiago de Cuba. They are evidence of the cruel treatment endured by enslaved people.

This mansion sits on a former sugar **plantation** in south-central Cuba. The enslaved people forced to work there made its owner the richest man in Cuba in the late 1700s.

Caribbean Base

Throughout the 16th and 17th centuries, Juana mainly served as a base for Spanish exploration. Ships stopped on the island for a short break and to restock supplies before carrying on to South and Central America. Other European nations, including England, France, and the Netherlands, vied for control of the Caribbean.

Havana became an important port for shipping between Spain and its colonies in the Americas. Gold, emeralds, and other goods were shipped to Havana from Central and South American mines. From there, they were sent to Spain. Cuba began to prosper—and it also caught the eye of pirates who wanted a piece of the action.

England attacked and occupied the city of Havana in its successful effort to take control of Cuba in 1762.

After controlling Cuba for almost one year, England gave it back to Spain in 1763 in exchange for Florida.

Sugar Rush

For the first two centuries of colonialism, most agricultural activities took place on small farms called haciendas. By the end of the 1700s, Cuba had garnered international attention for its thriving sugarcane industry. Around this time, there was turmoil on neighboring islands. Many plantation owners fled Haiti during the Haitian **Revolution**, in which enslaved people revolted against French colonial rule. These plantation owners brought their wealth and farming skills to Cuba.

At the time, there was also a global sugar shortage. The demand for sugar was high. But as the sugarcane industry grew in Cuba, so did the need for laborers. There were about 40,000 enslaved Africans in Cuba by the 1770s. That number skyrocketed to more than 400,000 by the 1840s. Enslaved people made up about a third of Cuba's population. Throughout the 1800s, more than half a million enslaved individuals were sent to Cuba, despite promises

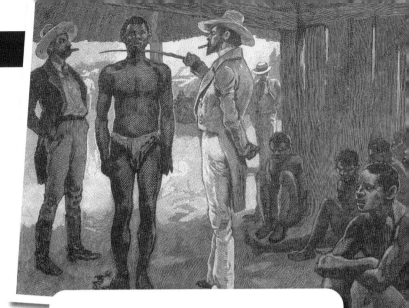

Even after Spain pledged to end its involvement in the slave trade in 1820, plantation owners insisted on continuing the practice. Hundreds of thousands of enslaved people were brought to plantations in the decades that followed.

by Spain's king to ban the trade of enslaved Africans in Spanish colonies. The slave trade ended in the mid-1860s, but it would take another two decades for enslavement to be abolished in Cuba.

The island's fertile soil and low-lying plains made it the ideal place for growing sugarcane.

The Cuban Fight for Independence

By the mid-1800s, Spain began to lose its hold on Cuba. More and more Cubans wanted freedom from colonial rule. They had lost faith in the Spanish government and wanted to make their own decisions for their country. Spain refused to listen to the people and even increased their taxes, making them more upset.

By 1868, the Cuban people had seen enough. A wealthy planter named Carlos Manuel de Céspedes took a stand. Known as the father of Cuban independence, Céspedes freed his enslaved laborers and called for the same for others. He then proclaimed independence for his country and incited a revolution. The Ten Years' War ended when Spain agreed to economic and political **reforms** for Cuba in 1878. However, Cuban independence had not yet been achieved.

From 1879 to 1880, *La Guerra Chiquita*, or The Little War, took place. It was, in many ways, a continuation of the Ten Years' War and was the second of three conflicts for Cuban independence.

A statue in Havana, Cuba, commemorates Carlos Manuel de Céspedes.

Calixto García, a Cuban general in all three uprisings

Martí was killed in action during the fighting, but his legacy lives on as a hero to the Cuban people.

Rising Up

In 1895, José Martí, a Cuban writer who was **exiled** to the United States, organized a third uprising. Spain sent large numbers of troops to Cuba to stop the uprising. However, Cuban generals Máximo Gómez and Antonio Maceo fought hard to maintain their position. Meanwhile, the United States kept tabs on the conflict. It had many business interests in Cuba and wanted to protect its assets and secure its trade relationship with the country.

U.S. Involvement

In 1898, the United States joined the war effort. The Spanish-American War lasted from April to August of that year. The Treaty of Paris between Spain and the United States was signed in December, granting Cuba independence from Spain. It also led to the U.S. **occupation** of Cuba from 1899 to 1902, while the new country recovered from the war and created a **constitution**. This was the beginning of a long and complicated relationship between Cuba and the United States.

This illustration depicts the Spanish surrender to the United States in Santiago de Cuba in July 1898.

Cuban Independence

Under the watchful eye of the United States, Cuba flourished. The economy, which had been in decline since the first independence movement, started to grow and sugar prices boomed. Thanks to its favorable climate and beautiful beaches, there was an increase in tourism to Cuba. This led to the development of hotels, restaurants, and casinos.

However, U.S. leaders favored political systems that prevented Afro-Cubans from having a voice. U.S. foreign investors owned much of the land and businesses in Cuba, giving them control over the economy. Even though Cuba was one of the wealthiest nations in Latin America by the mid-1900s, most Cubans lived in poverty. There was a large gap between the wealthy and the poor, especially in rural areas.

Years of living under the control of corrupt government leaders and U.S. **interventions** took their toll on the Cuban people.

During this period, much of the sugar industry was owned by U.S. investors. They controlled 70 percent of Cuba's arable land.

After successfully overthrowing the government, Castro became political leader of Cuba in 1959.

Time for Change

The Cuban people began to rise up against the government. A young lawyer and activist named Fidel Castro emerged during this time. He called on the courts to overthrow the government. When they did not, he took matters into his own hands.

Along with his brother Raúl, Castro established a **paramilitary** group called *El Movimiento*, or The Movement. They attempted a failed attack on the government on July 26, 1953. The Castro brothers received lengthy prison sentences for their part in the uprising, but they were freed and fled to Mexico. While there, they started the 26th of July Movement with Ernesto "Che" Guevara, a young revolutionary leader. Over the next few years, the men staged several attacks on the Cuban government as a part of the Cuban Revolution. Finally, Castro and his small rebel army overthrew the government on January 1, 1959.

Guevara also played a key role in the new Cuban government before his death in 1967. His image is well known today as a symbol of revolution.

25

Castro in Command

After Fidel Castro took control of the government, he aligned himself with the working class and poor. He got rid of **capitalism** and introduced a socialist system of government in its place. The idea was that all people should have equal opportunities by sharing in the wealth of the nation.

Castro was closely tied to the **Communist** Party of Cuba, which quickly took power over the country. In communist nations, the government has total control over prices, wages, housing, and all other aspects of life. The Cuban government began to take control of private property and businesses and **nationalized** them. It banned non-Cubans from operating businesses and encouraged sugarcane farmers to focus on food crops instead. The government became the country's largest employer.

Fidel Castro served as political leader from 1959 to 2008, before his brother Raúl took over. Raúl Castro stepped down in 2018.

Whether Cubans were employed as farmers, mechanics, doctors, or teachers, they most likely worked for government-run businesses.

In October 1962, the Cuban Missile Crisis threatened to escalate to nuclear war after the U.S. discovered Cuba had allowed the Soviet Union to install nuclear weapons on the island. Here, a Soviet ship loaded with missiles leaves Cuba after the crisis was resolved.

End of an Era

The Cuban government soon began to form alliances with the **Union of Soviet Socialist Republics** (U.S.S.R.), a communist regime. The U.S. government was opposed to communism and became concerned about Cuba's relationship with the Soviet Union. It started a **trade embargo** on all exports to Cuba, except food and medical supplies. Soon after, it also ended **diplomatic relations** with Cuba. As a result, Castro strengthened ties with the U.S.S.R.

Throughout the 1960s, the Cuban government continued to take control of businesses, daily life, and communication services in the country. Military leaders moved into high-ranking government positions. On top of that, faced with food shortages, the government imposed food rationing.

This rusty Soviet missile is one remnant of the Cuban Missile Crisis and Cuba's close relationship with the U.S.S.R.

The Goal of Equality

Havana had been the central focus of the colonial government. It received more economic support than other parts of the country, so hospitals, schools, roadways, electrical and water systems, and other **infrastructure** were far better in Havana than other parts of the country.

The new socialist regime, on the other hand, was tasked with making all parts of the country equal. It set up a **social welfare** system that provided free health care, public education, and government-supported housing. Infrastructure was built up in small towns and rural centers to bring their standards of living more closely in line with those found in Havana. Many of the wealthiest Cubans had fled to the United States after the Cuban Revolution. Their empty homes were given to the poor.

The Cuban government thought socialism would erase **racism** from the country. But racism runs deep within the country today, and Afro-Cubans rarely hold positions of power.

During the difficult period that followed the dissolution of the U.S.S.R., Cuba experienced an oil shortage. Some citizens resorted to using other forms of transportation when they could not fuel their cars.

Socialist Cuba

As Cuba became a socialist country, its dependence on the Soviet Union grew. Cuba relied heavily on economic and military aid from the U.S.S.R. That meant that when the U.S.S.R. dissolved in 1991, Cuba was impacted significantly. The country's economy spiraled, and poverty increased. While there have been some moderate changes to the Cuban government and businesses over the years, the state of the nation remains much the same today as it did in the mid-to-late 1900s.

The Soviet Union had been Cuba's main trading partner. This brought a lot of money into the country before the U.S.S.R.'s dissolution.

Law and Order

The Cuban constitution was established in 1976. It declared Cuba as an independent, socialist republic. The government maintains almost total control over every part of Cubans' lives. It is a one-party system headed by the Communist Party of Cuba.

The Cuban people elect the National Assembly of People's Power—but the candidates are preapproved by the Communist Party. The National Assembly of People's Power designates the president, vice president, and other members to the Council of Ministers.

The country is divided into 15 provinces and 168 **municipalities**. There is also one special municipality: Juventud Island. Provinces and municipalities have their own governments. They are overseen by the National Assembly of People's Power and the Communist Party. Many of their responsibilities overlap.

The National Assembly of People's Power also appoints members of the People's Supreme Court, which is the highest court in Cuba. District and regional courts are also part of Cuba's justice system. Municipal governments appoint judges to local courts. The law, although influenced by communist theory, is based on both the Spanish and American legal systems.

The government of Cuba restricts **civil liberties**, and people who speak out against the country's leadership are often arrested and treated unfairly.

Any Cuban citizen aged 16 and older can vote in elections.

por Cuba
Elecciones generales
2017-2018

Genuina demostración de democracia

The Cuban government does not allow independent media. It owns and controls all radio, TV, and newspaper outlets.

National Defense

There is a strong military presence in Cuba, with about 50,000 people serving in the army, navy, and air force and another 40,000 as **reservists**. Men between the ages of 16 and 50 are forced to serve a mandatory two-year term, but service is voluntary for women.

With an estimated 1 million reservists, the Territorial Troops Militia (MTT) is Cuba's largest paramilitary organization. It is mostly made up of women, seniors, and teenage boys. Their purpose is to serve alongside the military if a situation arises.

Cuba spends about $6 billion per year on its military.

Life in Cuba

Life in Cuba has its challenges. The social welfare system means that everyone has equal access to everything they need for survival. However, it also means there are tough restrictions on what citizens can access, outside of what the government gives them. Without support from the former Soviet Union, and with the ongoing trade embargo with the United States, just about everything is hard to come by in Cuba. From electricity blackouts and poor Internet services to food shortages and a lack of basic infrastructure, Cubans have learned to do more with less.

Housing

As a socialist country, the Cuban government is responsible for providing housing to everyone. However, it has not been able to meet the demand for new housing or keep existing housing in good condition. In 1960, a law was passed that aimed to eliminate the concept of landlords. This same law made it possible for Cubans to buy rental properties at a low cost. As a result, about 85 percent of Cubans own their homes. But many homeowners cannot afford to maintain their homes, and most are in disrepair.

Unemployment rates are low across Cuba. On average, people work an eight-hour day and get four weeks of paid vacation per year.

There are almost no Cubans who are unhoused, or who do not have homes.

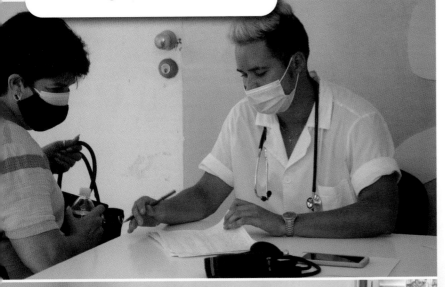

Doctors earn only about $60 per month, and they often work long hours in high-stress environments.

Health Care

The Cuban government provides free or low-cost universal health care for all. The country's health care system, in fact, is often said to be one of the best in the world, with high-quality medical professionals. But health care workers don't always have access to the resources they need to do their jobs well. At times, they might not have electricity, running water, or the pharmaceuticals, supplies, and advanced equipment that are readily available in some other nations.

Schools are well equipped in both cities and rural areas.

If a child does not have the means to travel to school, the Cuban government provides free food and accommodations.

Education

Education is free for everyone, from primary school to university. There are equal opportunities for all children, regardless of their gender or social status, and school is mandatory up to the ninth grade. Class sizes are restricted to 25 students or less to provide better learning opportunities. Many schools provide free before- and after-school care programs to accommodate working parents.

Getting Around

Cuba has an extensive highway system that connects cities and towns across the country. It consists of approximately 37,000 miles (60,000 km) of roadways. About 25,000 miles (40,000 km), however, are unpaved. *La Carretera Central*, or the Central Highway, is the most important in the country. It runs from one end of the main island to the other.

The country also has a public bus system, a railway for transporting sugarcane, and a small shipping fleet. Key ports include Cienfuegos, Havana, and Matanzas. Many major cities have airports that offer domestic flights to popular destinations across the country, including Varadero, Santiago de Cuba, and Baracoa.

Local Rides

Most Cubans do not own a car, so they rely on shared or public transportation to get around. *Camiones* are trucks that are turned into buses by adding boxes with benches or seats on the back. They are used to carry people, products, and even poultry along main highways and rural roads. The ride is cheap, costing up to $2 U.S. to travel 100 miles (160 km), but *camiones* are often hot and uncomfortable. *Collectivos* are another popular mode of transportation for locals. They are large classic cars that hold about seven people. They travel a fixed route between cities and towns and cost about $1 U.S. per 30 miles (50 km).

The José Martí International Airport in Havana is Cuba's main international airport.

There are 5,199 miles (8,367 km) of railroad tracks in Cuba. While public trains are available, they are slow and often experience delays and cancellations.

Getting to school or work in Havana often means hitching a ride.

Classic Cars

Cuba is well known for its colorful classic cars. However, what appears to be a cultural phenomenon to outsiders is evidence of the nation's internal struggles. During the Cuban Revolution, Castro banned the import of American cars to Cuba. The U.S. trade embargo also restricted the export of cars and parts to the island. With no new cars coming into the country, Cubans needed to find creative ways to keep any cars that were on the island in top shape. They became mechanics and used a mix and match of repurposed parts.

Today, the island is home to tens of thousands of vintage vehicles, and they are a top tourist attraction. But it was born out of necessity rather than as a fun way to draw people to the island. Restrictions on new car imports from Europe and Asia have been relaxed in recent years, but extremely high prices make it nearly impossible for the average Cuban to purchase one. A vehicle that sells for about $30,000 in the United States can cost more than $260,000 in Cuba.

The **ingenuity** and skill of Cuban mechanics has kept vintage cars on the road.

Almendrones are vintage car taxis that transport people around Havana.

35

A Vibrant Country

Food

Because food is rationed, special meals are rare. Most days, Cubans make do with what they have. *Desayuno*, or early breakfast, is the first meal of the day. It includes coffee with milk, fruit, and bread. The midday meal is called *almuerzo*, and it is made up of salad, fish, meat, eggs, vegetables, coffee, and dessert. Between 5 and 8 p.m., Cubans have their dinner, or *comida*, which includes many of the same foods as their midday meal. *Lechón asado*, a type of roast pork, is often served on special occasions.

One of the most common traditional foods in Cuba is called *ropa vieja*. It includes shredded meat cooked with tomatoes, onions, peppers, and cumin, served over rice. *Arroz con frijoles negros* is a popular side dish that's made from rice and beans. The Cubano sandwich is made from roast pork, ham, cheese, mustard, and pickles on crunchy Cuban bread. *Ajiaco*, an authentic Cuban soup, consists of a thick broth, shredded chicken, corn, potatoes, banana, pumpkin, onion, seasonings, and more.

Café cubano is a popular drink. It is made by pouring sweet cream over a strong espresso.

Ropa vieja is the national dish of Cuba.

The Cubano sandwich is a local favorite.

Cuban-born singer Celia Cruz was known as the Queen of Salsa.

Celebrations

Aside from Christmas, Christian holidays are not typically considered major events in Cuba. Most major Cuban celebrations are related to important historical events for the country. For example, Liberation Day festivities take place on January 1. The celebration honors the victory of the Cuban Revolution on that date in 1959. Another major celebration is National Rebellion Day, which takes place on July 26. It marks the date Fidel Castro led revolutionaries in an uprising in 1953.

Music and Dance

Cuban music is a mix of Latin American, African, and European influences. Music has an important role in the country's culture. Charanga, salsa, mambo, danzón, cha-cha, and rumba are a few of the traditional dance styles that are popular across Cuba. Performers can be found singing and dancing in clubs, on street corners, and in living rooms all over the country. The National Ballet of Cuba, established by famed Cuban ballerina Alicia Alonso, has also received international recognition.

May Day, or Labor Day, is celebrated on May 1 and honors Cuban workers.

CHAPTER 5

Literature

Cuban writers have developed a distinct literary style. In the early 1800s, they often wrote about colonialism, enslavement, and the mixing of cultures. The 1882 novel *Cecilia Valdés* by Cirilo Villaverde is an important example of this kind of work. Later, Cubans wrote about revolution and independence. José Martí, one of Cuba's best-known authors, wrote essays encouraging Cubans to fight for their freedom. He also wrote poems about anti-**imperialism** and Cuban independence.

Art

Art is an important part of culture in Cuba. The country helps develop artistic talents through various schools, support programs, and organizations, such as the Cuban Film Institute and the National Cultural Council. The Cuban government created the Universidad de las Artes, or University of the Arts, in Havana in 1976. The university offers programs in music, visual arts, theater, dance, media, and preservation and conservation.

Handmade Cuban cigars are renowned around the world. Rolling them is considered a traditional Cuban art form. It has been passed down for generations.

There are about 400 public libraries and 250 museums across Cuba. The Museo Nacional de Bellas Artes, or National Museum of Fine Arts, features Cuban artists.

Sports

Sports are a major pastime in Cuba. Cubans enjoy playing everything from soccer to volleyball and boxing. Baseball is the national sport and the most popular across the country. Cuban baseball teams often perform well at international events, such as the Olympics and Pan American Games. Top athletes are often celebrated as national heroes. Young athletes with extraordinary skills can attend government-run boarding schools to develop their talents while still doing their regular studies.

Clothing

Lightweight, loose-fitting clothing made from breathable fabrics is best suited to Cuba's warm, subtropical climate. Most people wear Western-style clothing, such as T-shirts, day to day. Traditional clothing is casual and relaxed. It includes *guayabera* shirts for men, which have four pockets and buttons on the front and two sets of pleats that run vertically down the front and back. Women wear colorful, long dresses that have wide, tiered skirts and off-the-shoulder necklines.

Many men wear Panama hats for Sun protection. They are similar to fedoras and made from straw.

Traditional Cuban dresses are colorful and vibrant. Women often wear colorful wraps on their heads as well.

Many Cuban children participate in baseball leagues. The sport is a central part of national pride for many Cubans.

Looking to the Future

Cubans today continue to live in a time warp created by strict U.S. trade restrictions and the collapse of the U.S.S.R. They live in a place where the government controls their daily lives and prevents them from being active members in the fast-paced, ever-changing world around them.

From the historical importance of agriculture to the role of tourism as a leading Cuban industry, Cuba's land and environment has a deep impact on how its people earn their income and develop their identities and culture. Urban development, economic growth, and environmental conservation all depend on the connection between people and the land.

Cuba was forced to adapt when faced with food and oil shortages. One solution is urban farming, in which food is grown within urban areas such as Havana. The practice has helped increase affordable food supply and promotes sustainability in how land is used for farming.

Tourism

Since the collapse of the U.S.S.R., travel and tourism has become a fast-growing industry in Cuba. Throughout the 1990s, Cuba placed an emphasis on tourism to generate income and repair the crumbling economy. Along with the help of foreign investors, many new hotels and resorts were built in popular areas. Today, tourism is one of the country's main sources of revenue.

Approximately 4 million people visit Cuba each year, mainly from Canada and Europe. The vibrant culture, historic buildings, and beautiful beaches are some of the main tourist draws. Another big draw is the country's pristine coral reef system, which is one of the healthiest marine ecosystems in the Caribbean. It makes for some of the best diving experiences in the region. As more tourists visit Cuba, however, the reefs are put at greater risk. The government has programs in place to ensure their protection.

A large number of Cubans flock to tourist areas where they can work in the tourism industry and add tips to their incomes.

Cuba's 263 protected areas make up about 22 percent of its total land.

With its high number of doctors and effective health care system, Cuba was able to respond to COVID-19 effectively and keep death rates low, compared to other Caribbean countries.

U.S. Relations

In 2015, U.S. President Barack Obama worked with Raúl Castro to begin relaxing trade restrictions, opening the door to a renewed relationship between the two countries and a brighter future for the Cuban people. However, a few years later, U.S. President Donald Trump once again imposed severe sanctions on Cuba, forcing the relationship several steps backward. In 2022, U.S. President Joe Biden once again began to ease some restrictions, but it has not been not enough to pull Cuba out of its economic crisis. As a result, Cuba continues to experience limited trade opportunities.

Cuba relies on food imports, which declined during the Trump administration and even further when the COVID-19 pandemic began.

COVID-19 Pandemic

The COVID-19 pandemic further deepened Cuba's economic struggles. Tourism came to a crashing halt, leaving the country without one of its main income sources. Food lines grew even longer, power outages became more frequent, and the government began charging for some goods in foreign currencies, making them even harder for the average person to buy.

Distribución de la sal

Consumidores	1 vuelta	2 vuelta	3 vuelta	Total Trimes
1~2	1	---	---	1
3~4	1	1	---	2
5~6	1	1	1	3
7~10	2	2	1	5
11~13	2	2	2	6
14~16	3	2	2	7
17 y mas	3	3	2	8

Religion

During the Cuban Revolution, Castro declared Cuba an atheist country. Atheism is a disbelief in any god or gods. Cubans had no religious freedom. The ban on religion was removed in the 1990s, and people were allowed to openly practice their religious beliefs. However, there are still some restrictions on religious practices. For instance, churches cannot run schools or hospitals, and religious events are closely monitored. Catholicism is the main religion, but many people also practice Afro-Cuban religions that are a blend of African and Catholic customs, such as Santería.

Santería ceremonies often involve dancing, chanting, and drumming.

Santería developed in Cuba from the beliefs of enslaved Africans. It is estimated that a majority of Cubans practice Santería in some way.

Some estimates say that Catholicism is the predominant religion in Cuba, with up to 60 percent of the population identifying as Catholic.

Mass Demonstrations

In 2018 and 2021, Miguel Díaz-Canel became president of Cuba and leader of the Communist Party following Raúl Castro's retirement. He is the first person to hold the post that does not bear the Castro name, though he was handpicked by Castro as his successor.

While Díaz-Canel has pointed to the United States as the source of the country's problems, there is more to the story. Young Cubans want political reforms, and they are not willing to wait in silence. On July 11, 2021, thousands of people took to the streets across Cuba in one of the country's largest mass protests ever. Despite the fact that anti-government demonstrations are illegal in Cuba, protesters demanded freedom, risking arrest or worse. The government responded by setting up counterprotests, shutting down the Internet, and sending in special forces to control the growing crowds.

Calling for a new system of government and better quality of life, protesters in Cuba and other places, such as Florida (above), chanted that Díaz-Canel should step down.

Hundreds of activists were detained and given long prison sentences after the protest. Countries such as the U.S. have called for their release.

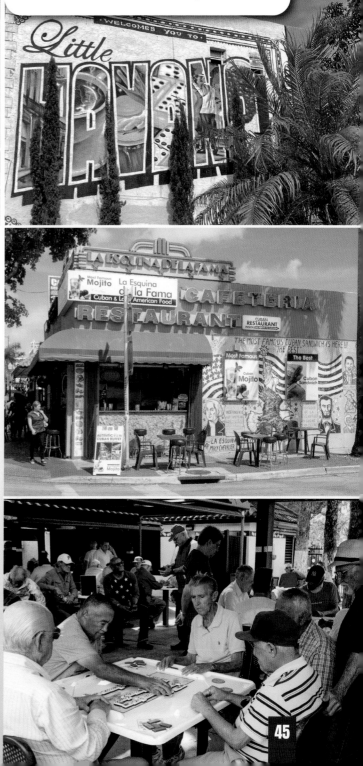

Many Cuban immigrants and exiles, or those who fled Cuba after the 1959 Revolution, made their homes in the neighborhood of Little Havana in Miami, Florida. Little Havana is bursting with Cuban culture and is known for its food, street life, music, and friendly residents.

The minimum wage in Cuba is not enough for most people to survive, even with subsidized food, housing, and social welfare programs.

Moving On

Older Cubans remember a time where the government provided for them in exchange for their support. In those days, the idea of a peaceful socialist society where everyone was equal seemed like a realistic goal. But times have been especially tough since the collapse of the Soviet Union and Cuba's economic decline in the 1990s.

Cuba struggles to produce enough income to purchase the necessary goods for its people, and the gap between rural and urban life has widened. The idea of equality for everyone is a distant memory. While many older Cubans still support socialism, younger Cubans want more freedoms. It's difficult to predict what will come of the nation in a post-Castro era. Many young people are choosing to leave if given the opportunity, and Cuba's population is starting to decline as a result. Though its culture is vibrant, Cuba has an uncertain future.

arable Land that is suitable for growing crops

archipelago A chain or group of islands in an area

black market Unregulated economic activity in which goods are bought and sold illegally

capitalism An economic system in which private citizens own, produce, and sell goods for profit

cays Low islands made mostly of sand or coral

civil liberties Rights and freedoms protected by a country's laws

climate change A long-term change in the temperatures and weather patterns on Earth. Climate change often refers to global warming, the rise in global temperatures due to human activity.

colonial Relating to a colony, or a country or area occupied by and under the control of another country

commercial Relating to buying and selling goods

communist Related to communism, an economic and political system in which goods and resources are owned commonly, usually by government, rather than by private individuals

conquistador A Spanish leader, or conqueror, in the colonization of the Americas

constitution A country's basic principles and laws

diplomatic relations The arrangements or relationships between countries, carried out by representatives, or diplomats

encomienda A system in which Spanish colonists were given land and the right to demand forced labor from the Indigenous peoples who inhabited it

exiled Being barred from one's country, often for political reasons

fertile Land that is able to grow plants

gypsum A mineral often used as fertilizer and in types of plaster, chalk, and drywall

imperialism A country's practice of exerting power over outside territories

Indigenous The original inhabitants of a place

infrastructure The systems and services that help a society operate, such as roads and power plants

ingenuity Inventive and able to solve problems creatively

interventions Involvement of one party, such as a country, in another party's affairs

karst A landscape made up of limestone and containing caves, sinkholes, and other formations

marine reserve Areas of the sea that are protected

municipalities Cities or towns with their own governments

nationalize To transfer control and ownership of a business, industry, or land to a national government

occupation The military control of one country or territory by another

paramilitary Forces that are not part of a country's official military, but often operate in a similar way. Sometimes, paramilitary units complete tasks that the official military or police cannot.

plantation A large farm on which crops are grown for profit

port A town or city on a coast where ships can load and unload cargo

racism Beliefs, actions, and systems of power that are rooted in the idea that a person's race determines their traits and capabilities, and that one race is superior

rations Limited amounts or portions that a person is allowed to have

reforms Changes made to improve something

reservists Soldiers who are not serving in the regular army, but can be called on to fight if needed

revolution A sudden and complete change, especially the overthrow of a government

slave trade The capturing, buying, and selling of enslaved people

social welfare Organized government or privately run services to help people meet their needs

socialist Related to socialism, an economic and political system in which resources are shared equally and allocated by an elected government

submarine terraces Flat, step-like structures under the sea

subsidies Money provided by government to assist a person, business, or industry

subtropical The regions north and south of the tropical zones on the equator. Subtropical climates are often hot in summer and mild in winter.

territorial Relating to territories, or areas that are controlled by a country or ruler

trade embargo A ban on exporting and importing goods and services to and from a certain country

tributaries A river or stream that flows into a larger river or lake

UNESCO World Heritage Site A protected landmark or area singled out by the United Nations Educational, Scientific, and Cultural Organization (UNESCO) as being globally significant

Union of Soviet Socialist Republics A former communist country (1922–1991), also known as the Soviet Union, that included a large portion of eastern Europe and northern Asia

Books

Cuevas, Adrianna. *Cuba in My Pocket*. Farrar, Straus and Giroux, 2021.

Green, Jen. *Countries of the World: Cuba*. National Geographic Children's Books, 2007.

Hyde, Natalie. *The Cold War and the Cuban Missile Crisis*. Crabtree Publishing, 2016.

Manzano, Sonia. *Coming Up Cuban*. Scholastic, 2022.

Websites

www.nationsonline.org/oneworld/cuba.htm
Check out the links compiled on this website for more detailed information about Cuba, from its UNESCO World Heritage Sites to its celebrated national ballet.

www.miamiandbeaches.com/neighborhoods/little-havana
Explore the information, photos, and videos on this website to learn all about the history and lively Cuban culture of Little Havana, Miami.

kids.nationalgeographic.com/geography/countries/article/cuba
Learn all about Cuba's geography, people, and history, and click through the vibrant images on this National Geographic site.

www.pbs.org/wgbh/americanexperience/features/comandante-pre-castro-cuba/
Discover more about the history of Cuba before Castro's 1959 revolution, which changed life for Cubans forever.

About the Author

Heather C. Hudak has written hundreds of kids' books on all kinds of topics. She loves to travel when she's not writing. Heather has visited about 60 countries and hopes to travel to others one day.